Let's Write

Monsters and Spooky Creatures

31 Creative Writing Prompts

by Melissa Gijsbers

©2025 Melissa Gijsbers
melissagijsbers.com

Finish This Book Press

Written by Melissa Gijsbers

Cover Design using elements from Canva

ISBN: 978-1-7641755-1-7

All rights reserved. Apart from any permitted use under the Copyright Act, no part of this book may be reproduced, copied, scanned, stored in a retrieval system, recorded or transmitted in any form or by any means, without the prior permission of the publisher.

Dedication

To Victoria, who can add werewolves to any writing prompt I set!

Table of Contents

Dedication iii

Introduction 1

Melissa's Golden Rules of Writing 3

Tips on how to use Writing Prompts 5

Writing Prompts 6

Conclusion 37

About the Author 38

Also by Melissa Gijsbers: 40

Introduction

Welcome writers,

So many people say that to be a writer, you need to write every day. This isn't something I believe. I believe that to be a writer, you need to write. That said, writing every day can be useful as it helps you practice your writing and make progress on whatever you are working on.

One thing that I love to do is play around with writing prompts and see what happens. I get one and write, purely for the joy of writing. Sometimes, these stories turn into something I want to develop into a piece that can be entered in a competition or published, but most of the time, it's simply fun to write. I can let go of any of my worries that I'm not good enough or that not one will enjoy it because I'm simply in the moment and writing for myself.

This is what the *Let's Write* series of books is all about.

Each book contains 31 writing prompts, enough for one a day for a month, with a few extra if you are choosing a month without 31 days. You can also use them at random when you want to write something but don't know where to start.

Each book has a theme; this one is all about monsters and spooky creatures. I know there are lot of people who love horror movies, especially around Halloween, I'm not one of them, however I do enjoy having fun writing about spooky characters. You can use these prompts to write something on any part of the spectrum of spooky stories. They can simply be about the monsters and characters, or you can turn them into something scary that fits perfectly in the horror genre. Have fun with them and be creative.

Once you've finished all the prompts in this book, be sure to look out for some of the others in this series or go back and play with them again.

Happy Writing.

Melissa Gijsbers

Melissa's Golden Rules of Writing

1. **Have FUN!** - creative writing is all about the process. After all, if you're not having fun, what's the point?
2. **It's YOUR Story**—write your story your way. There is no single way to write a story, so experiment, play, and write whatever comes to mind.
3. **Experiment**—play with different styles and genre. You never know what you'll enjoy writing until you try. Plus, you don't have to limit yourself to just one type of writing.
4. **Try something new**—if your story isn't working, try something new. A different point of view, style, genre, or even a new prompt if the one you're working on isn't working!
5. **Have FUN!** - Did I mention have fun? Whether you are writing something silly or serious, creating a story is fun, so enjoy it.
6. **Write as long or as short as you like**—If you only have a few minutes, then you can write something short. It doesn't matter if you don't

finish a story or piece of writing in a sitting, or at all.

7. **First drafts are meant to be crappy***—this is something many people don't realise, it's no issue if your first draft is not perfect. Everything can be fixed up in the editing process.

8. **You don't have to finish**—if you're writing for fun, and you don't finish your story, that's okay. You can always come back and finish it another time.

9. **Have FUN!** - I may have mentioned this before... have fun writing your story, poem, or whatever else you're writing.

* Crappy = flawed, imperfect, incomplete, not up to scratch, unsatisfactory

Tips on how to use Writing Prompts

1. **Read the prompt carefully**— What is it asking you to do?
2. **Think outside the box**— Is there a way you can use the prompt in a fun or unusual way?
3. **Use the prompt more than once**— If you have more than one idea, then write them down. You can use a prompt in many different ways. You can save them to use next year, or even after Christmas if you get in a story writing mood.
4. **Just write**— Don't worry about titles, spelling, grammar, or anything else, just write. This is a first draft. Underline any words you're not sure about spelling and you can come back to them later. Everything can be fixed up in the editing process.
5. **Read over what you've written**— When you've done, read over what you've written and fix up any obvious errors. Then you can have fun editing your story to share (if you want to).

Writing Prompts

1

Write a story about Halloween, from the point of view of a ghost, witch, monster, or other spooky creature

2

Write a story about a mum who doesn't notice there is a ghost in the house causing chaos because she blames it all on her kids

3

First line: For most people, the number 13 is an unlucky number, but for me, it's number 9

4

Write a story about the monster under your bed

5

Write a story about a vampire going to the dentist

6

You are in the museum, and a mummy comes to life.

Write a story about what happens next

7

Write an ode to all things spooky

8

Write a story about an unconventional witch, ghost, or other spooky being

9

Write a spooky story using these random words:

Rainbow, Lamp, Pillow, Chocolate, Footpath

10

You wake up in the middle of the night and find a crying ghost sitting on the end of your bed. Write a story about what happens next

11

Write a story with the following first line:

There is a monster under the bed of every child. The monster under my bed wasn't quite what I expected it to be...

12

There is a doll in your house that moves to a new position every night. Write the story where you find out it's moving on its own!

13

You move into a house next to a graveyard.

Every Halloween, there's a party next door.

Write a story about the party in the graveyard

14

Write a story about the troll that lives under the bridge in the local park

15

Write a story about a ghost living alone in an abandoned haunted house

16

It's Halloween, and you've made a jack-o-lantern to decorate your porch.

Imagine the jack-o-lantern starts speaking to you. What does it say?

17

Write a story about a Halloween decorating competition, where a spooky creature is the judge

18

Write a story about a witch who always gets her spells just a little bit wrong

19

Zed is a zombie who doesn't like walking.

Write a story about his day

20

Write a spooky story set in a shopping centre, with a werewolf going Christmas shopping

21

One day, you discover your boss, or your teacher, is a werewolf.

Write a story about your discovery

22

You are moving house, and the town you are in is full of spooky creatures.

Write a story about settling in

23

Imagine you are a vampire, trying to live in the modern world. Write a story about navigating life

24

Write a story about a vegetarian vampire

25

One day a monster steals your homework, or your child's homework.

Write a letter to the school to explain what has happened

26

Typically, witches ride on brooms, but things have changed in this modern era.

Write something about the latest transport for witches

27

Write a story about a ghost who lives in the library so that they can finally finish all the books on their 'to be read' pile

28

Write a story about a spider that lives in a house who continually plots ways to scare the homeowners, with varying results

29

Write a story about a non-black cat that is bad luck

30

There are some interesting inscriptions on tomb stones.

Write an inscription for a fictional character

31

Write a story with the following last line:

From this day, Wendy the Witch knew never to use a stainless-steel cauldron ever again!

Conclusion

I hope you've had fun with these writing prompts and enjoyed crafting stories.

One fantastic thing about writing prompts is that you can use them more than once and come out with an entirely different story.

If you do want to use the prompt again and aren't quite sure what to do, try writing from a different point of view, or a different style or genre than you did last time. You can also put this book away for a while and try them all again with a fresh mind.

Try it and see what happens.

If you enjoyed the prompts in this book, be sure to check out the other books in this series as well as my other writing prompt books.

Happy Writing,

Melissa Gijsbers

About the Author

Melissa Gijsbers is an author and booklover. Stories have always been a big part of her life, and she has been writing them for as long as she can remember.

She started working with young writers in 2013 at the Monash Public Library and has been inspiring them to write by providing them with crazy writing prompts ever since! This group helped Melissa discover how important creative writing can be for wellbeing, and how much fun writing prompts can be.

Her first book, *Swallow Me, NOW!* was published in 2014. Since then, she has published more books and written even more stories that may or may not be published.

She currently lives in Gippsland in Victoria, Australia and spends quite a bit of time coming up with fun writing ideas for stories, as well as writing more books herself.

You can find out more about Melissa and her books on her website—
www.melissagijsbers.com

Also by Melissa Gijsbers:

Writing Prompt Books

- Genie in my Drink Bottle & other writing prompts
- Great Lost Sock Mystery & other writing prompts
- Writing Prompts – Random Words
- Let's Write – Flowers, Plants & Gardens

Other books

- Swallow Me, NOW!
- 3… 2… 1… Done!
- Lizzy's Dragon
- Lilly's Library
- My Princess Wears a Superhero Cape
- My Mummy is Evil
- Stories Through the Rainbow short story collection
- Creative Writing for Wellbeing
- Active Books for ADHD

www.ingramcontent.com/pod-product-compliance
Lightning Source LLC
Chambersburg PA
CBHW071917070526
44583CB00016B/2035